KNOW YOUR SPORT

Cycling
Paul Mason

SEA-TO-SEA
Mankato Collingwood London

This edition first published in 2010 by
Sea-to-Sea Publications
Distributed by Black Rabbit Books
P.O. Box 3263, Mankato, Minnesota
56002

Copyright © Sea-to-Sea Publications
2010

Printed in USA

Mason, Paul, 1967-
  Cycling / Paul Mason.
      p. cm. -- (Know your sport)
  Includes index.
  ISBN 978-1-59771-218-7 (hardcover)
  1. Cycling--Juvenile literature. I. Title.
  GV1043.5.M353 2010
  796.6--dc22
                                    2008045014

9 8 7 6 5 4 3 2

Published by arrangement with the Watts
Publishing Group Ltd., London

Series editor: Jeremy Smith
Art director: Jonathan Hair
Series designed and created for
Franklin Watts by Storeybooks.
Designer: Rita Storey
Editor: Nicola Edwards
Photography: Tudor Photography,
  Banbury

Note: At the time of going to press, the
statistics and player profiles in this book were
up to date. However, due to some players'
active participation in the sport, it is possible
that some of these may now be out of date.

Picture credits
© Geoff Waugh/Alamy p18; © Jacky
Naegelen/Reuters/Corbis p14, © Tim de
Waele/Corbis p22, © Troy Wayrynen/
NewSport/Corbis p21(top); istock pp 6,
7(bottom), 8(right), 9(top), 11(right) and 19;
Paul Mason pp 7(top), 11(left) 26 and 27.

Every attempt has been made to clear
copyright. Should there be any inadvertent
omission please apply to the publisher
for rectification.

Cover images: Tudor Photography, Banbury.

All photos posed by models.
Thanks to Matt Gittings, Emma Pitt, Sam
Serruya, and Cameron Swarbrick.

The Publisher would like to thank Adrian Pitt
and the Palmer Park Velo Cycling Club for all
their help.

Taking part in sports
is a fun way to get in shape, but
like any form of physical
exercise, it has an element of
risk, particularly if you are unfit,
overweight, or suffer from any
medical conditions. It is
advisable to consult a healthcare
professional before beginning
any program
of exercise.

Contents

What is Cycling?

"Now that," said the famous adventurer and writer Jack London, "is something that makes life worth living!" He was talking about cycling, one of the world's most popular kinds of exercise.

Cycling as Transportation

Cycling is not only a form of exercise, but also a form of transportation for millions of people around the world. In many cities, a bike is by far the fastest way to get around.

Cyclists can use special cycle lanes, and whiz past the lines of cars sitting stuck in traffic jams.

A bike is a much less expensive way of getting around than a car. And unlike motorized transportation, bikes do not pump harmful pollution into the air every time they are used.

Bike Racing

Ever since bicycles were invented, people have been racing on them. But bike racing first became famous around the world in

Riding a bike—like any exercise—helps your body work better, keeps sickness at bay, keeps your weight down, and can even help you do better at school!

▼

The péloton (main group of riders) of the Tour de France—the world's most famous bike race—sweeps through Kent's countryside in England in June 2007. The Tour often visits other countries, but most of the racing happens in France.

1903. That year the toughest bike race on Earth, the Tour de France, was first run. The Tour lasted 19 days, and often covered 250 miles (400km) in a day. The racers often had to carry on riding into the night to finish each day's distance.

Today, the Tour is still the most famous of road races, but there are many other kinds of bike racing, too. Cross-country, BMX, downhill, and endurance racing are all increasingly popular.

The First Bicycles

Early bikes had solid "tires," which made them very uncomfortable! They also had a giant front wheel and a tiny rear. They were called "penny-farthings," after large (penny) and small (farthing) coins used in Britain at the time. Then, in the late 1800s, bikes more like today's began to appear. The wheels were the same size, and the bikes had air-filled tires. These new bikes were much easier and more comfortable to ride, and by 1900 a craze for cycling had spread around the world. Now, everyone can join in the fun.

The First Round-the-World Rider

In 1884, Thomas Stevens rode a penny-farthing from the West to the East Coast of the USA. Then, between 1885 and 1886 he carried on, from London, through Europe, the Middle East, China, and Japan, to become the first cyclist to ride around the world.

The Best Bike for You

It's important to get the right kind and size of bike, whether you use it for racing, traveling around, or to stay in shape—otherwise you will not enjoy riding it. The bike you choose needs to be set up so that it's comfortable and transfers all your pedaling effort into speed.

The Right Kind of Bike

Riding the right type of bike makes cycling much more enjoyable. There are many different kinds, including:

- Mountain bikes, which can be ridden anywhere but are relatively slow on the road.
- Road bikes, which have skinny wheels and tires, and are very light. They are good on the road, but not too good off of it.
- Cyclocross bikes, which are basically road bikes with fatter, knobbled tires. These are almost as quick as road bikes on the road, and can be used for easy off-road riding as well.
- Specialist bikes such as BMX and all-terrain mountain bikes are not ideal for general-purpose use.

This time-trial rider is on an ultra-modern, carbon-framed time-trial bike. The riding position is very uncomfortable for long periods, so the bike is only really suitable for short, fast rides.

These mountain-bike riders are on specialized full-suspension all-terrain bikes.

The right size frame
When your feet are on the ground, you need a gap of 1–4 inches (3–10cm) between your body and the top tube here.

Saddle angle
The saddle is usually most comfortable when it is parallel to the ground. Some riders even use a level to make sure it's exactly flat.

Saddle height
When you sit on the saddle with your heel on the pedal at its lowest point, your knee should be have a slight bend.

Chain

Handlebars
Higher handlebars are usually more comfortable. Lower handlebars are more aerodynamic and allow a higher speed. It is best to start with the handlebars about level with the saddle, and make adjustments from there.

It is important to have a good, strong lock for your bike.

A bike that has been set up well will be comfortable and more fun to ride.

Setting up Your Bike

Setting up your bike means adjusting the saddle height and handlebars to find the best riding position for you. A bike that is set up well travels faster, because it transfers your pedaling power to the back wheel efficeintly. Badly setup bikes cause injuries to your knees or back.

People adjust their bike setup to suit the kind of riding they are doing: racing bike and BMX riders have the saddle height very low, road racers have it set high. The photo guide on this page gives you a good place to start.

Safety Checks

Check your bike regularly to make sure it is safe:
• Do the brakes respond properly?
• Are the handlebars completely secure?
• Is the saddle also secure?
• Are the wheels fastened as tightly as possible?

Clothing and Safety

It's possible to cycle wearing almost anything. Some people even like to pedal along wearing nothing at all—a few towns have recently started holding naked bicycle rides! Assuming you do decide to wear clothes, though, a bit of thought about what you put on makes cycling a lot more comfortable and safer.

Ideal Bike Clothing

The best clothes for cycling are quite tight fitting. Loose clothes are generally a bad idea because once you get up to speed, they flap around and get in the way. This is especially true with legwear: if flapping material gets caught up in your bike chain, disaster can rapidly follow!

Cyclists who insist on the baggy, grunge look often wear shorts instead of long

Helmet

Cycling glasses protect the rider's eyes.

Stretchy top is warm but doesn't get sweaty.

Gloves cushion the rider's hands.

A well equipped young rider.

Waterproof jacket can be rolled up small and stored in the back pocket of the top.

Stretchy shorts with special padding where they touch the saddle.

Special shoes can be pressed into pedals to clip onto them. Most riders find they can go faster using this type of shoe and pedal.

pants. Shorts are cooler and more comfortable in everything but the coldest weather, and even the baggiest ones can't get caught up in your chain!

Being Seen

Cycling on busy roads can be dangerous, and it is important to make sure that drivers see you in plenty of time. That way, they can either slow down or steer around you. Many cyclists choose to wear bright colors, and at night something reflective, so that they are lit up brightly by a vehicle's headlights. At night it is also crucial to have bright lights on the front and back of the bike.

This rider will be easy for car drivers to see!

▼

Having a bell means you can warn people you are coming up behind them. This is very handy if there are walkers around, because they often forget to check if a bike is coming before stepping into the road.

▲

It's Better by Bike!

At the huge Mercedes Benz car factory in Germany, what do the workers use to get from department to department? What else? Bicycles!

Fitness and Training

Cycling is a great way of getting into shape, because it is easy to work it into your normal daily routine. Instead of being driven to school, you can go on your bike. (You might even persuade your mom or dad to come along for the ride!)

Fitness Benefits

There are many benefits to getting fit:

- It makes your bones, heart, lungs, and every muscle in your body stronger.
- Studies show that children who do regular exercise do better at school.
- Health problems such as back pain, sleeplessness, and digestive problems are helped by exercise.

Cycling is particularly good because it can be done at any pace. Even very unfit people can go cycling, starting slowly and building up speed as they get fitter.

Joining a Cycling Club

If you become serious about cycling and aim to take part in competitions, the best way to improve your fitness and technique is to join an official cycling club. A club is also somewhere to meet up with other young cyclists, and try all the different kinds of styles of cycling until you find the one that's best for you.

Training Together

At a cycling club, the riders train together, pushing each other to higher fitness levels than they could achieve on their own. When you ride as a group, there's always someone

Next time you're going somewhere, ask yourself, "Could I go on my bike instead?" The answer is usually yes, because almost any trip under a few miles long can be made by bike.

Cycling's First Superstar

Englishman James Moore (1849–1935) is said to have won the first-ever bike race, in 1868 in France. That same year, he also won the first-ever Paris-Rouen race. Cycling wasn't as well paid then, and Moore had to pay his own train fare home from Rouen. Not only that, his bike was stolen from outside a café near the finishing line!

who races away from the front, forcing everyone else to keep up!

Working with a Coach

One of the big advantages of joining a cycling club is that you get to work with a qualified coach. A good coach will be able to give you advice on just about any aspect of cycling, including:

- What kind of competition he or she thinks you are best at (road, track, mountain bike, etc.).
- Your riding style and technique.
- The best way to set your bike up.
- Training, and other fitness issues, such as the best foods to eat.

Choosing a Club

It is a good idea to pick the club you join carefully, because not all clubs specialize in every kind of cycling. If you are already interested in, for example, mountain biking, check that the club has other mountain-biking members and a mountain-bike coach.

Cycling clubs aren't just about training—they're usually a good place to make friends, too.

Young cyclists working with their coach, who is explaining the training he wants them to do.

Setting off on a training ride together.

You are never too young to get involved.

Cadence and Gears

"Cadence" means pedaling speed. Pedaling at the right speed is an essential cycling skill. Finding your ideal cadence improves your long-distance endurance and uphill riding.

Pedaling Speed

The speed you pedal at makes a big difference to your cycling. Pedaling too slowly is hard work, and tires you out quickly. Pedaling too fast means you end up traveling more slowly than you need to, without putting enough pressure on the pedals. All riders pedal at a slightly different cadence, but aiming for one pedal stroke per second is a good place to start.

Shifting Technique

To keep your cadence at one pedal revolution per second, you need to be in the right gear (see page 15). Shifting gear smoothly is a skill:

1) Make sure you can find the gear shift levers with your fingers without looking at them. Keep your eyes on where you are going!
2) Ease off the pressure on the pedals slightly. Keep them turning, but do not press down hard.
3) Quickly shift gear. Don't put full pressure on the pedals until the gear has completely changed.

Lance Armstrong

Date of Birth: September 18th, 1971

Nationality: American

Probably the world's most famous cyclist, Lance won the biggest race of all, the Tour de France, a record seven times between 1999 and 2005. He also won 22 stages of the race— most professional cyclists can only dream of winning even one! After fighting off cancer he will be making a historic comeback to professional cycling in 2009.

Lance was famous among cyclists for his unusually high cadence, which he felt helped him ride better in the mountains and time trials than almost anyone else.

Lance Armstrong of the U.S. cycles toward the finish line to win the 16th stage of the Tour de France.

Shifting Gear

1 On flat ground, the rider will probably be in one of her middle gears: the chain will be on one of the middle cogs on the back wheel.

2 As the rider starts to go uphill, she shifts to a lower gear, with the chain on a bigger cog on the back wheel. This lower gear is easier to pedal.

3 Coming downhill, the rider shifts to a higher gear, with the chain on a small cog on the back wheel. The bike is harder to pedal, but gravity is helping to pull it downward!

▲ Picking the right gear for the type of slope you are riding on makes cycling quicker and easier.

Some bikes now have shifters that allow you to change two or three gears at a time. This can be very useful if a hill turns out to be a lot steeper than you expected!

Using Gears

Using the right gear allows you to keep pedaling at one revolution per second, whether you are going uphill, downhill, or along flat ground.

- The lowest gear is the one that's easiest to pedal. On flat ground, a low gear has you spinning the pedals like crazy, just to go along at walking speed. But for riding up steep hills, low gears are a cyclist's biggest friend.

- A high gear is much harder to pedal, and would be impossible to use going up a steep hill. For coming DOWN a steep hill, though, they are great!

Most riders use a middle gear most of the time.

Uphill Riding Skills

One of the things many people starting out in cycle racing hate is riding uphill. A few coaching tips can make cycling uphill much easier— some people even end up enjoying it!

Uphill Cadence

Many riders find it is a good idea to pedal at a slightly higher cadence (pedaling speed) than normal when going uphill. This saves energy, and means that if the slope ahead gets steeper they will be able to carry on without having to change gear. A high cadence is particularly useful when riding uphill off-road. Here, obstacles such as rocks and tree roots can easily slow the bike down or throw you off balance.

To Stand, or Not to Stand?

Some riders achieve extra power by standing on the pedals and rocking the handlebars from side to side. This adds a quick burst of speed. It is important, though, to make sure the bike does not start

1 *As the riders approach the hill, they pick what they think will be the right gear to help them get up the slope.*

2 *The riders sitting down have picked the right gear and can ride with a good body position. They are sitting down, their weight is forward on the bike and their elbows bent. The bike will be easy to pedal in a straight line.*

zigzagging across the road—you should keep the wheels pointing straight uphill.

Standing up on the pedals drains a rider's energy far more than sitting on the saddle and pedaling steadily. It is a technique that should only be used in short bursts, such as to catch up during a race.

Body Position

The main photo sequence shows a good uphill riding body position. The seated riders

Speedy Eagle

Possibly the greatest uphill racer ever is the Spanish rider Federico Bahamontes. Bahamontes climbed so high, so fast that he was called the "Eagle of Toledo."

will be able to reach the top of a slope in much better shape than the rider who is standing up.

3 *Farther up the slope, the rider standing on the pedals starts to fall back. He has used up too much energy pedaling in a high gear, and cannot keep up.*

This rider has terrible technique. As he pulls on the handlebars, the wheels zig and zag from side to side, meaning he cycles farther than if he was traveling in a straight line.

Downhill Riding Skills

Downhill mountain-bike races are among the most exciting bike events to take part in, and the most spectacular to watch. The skills and techniques of the riders, at speeds where a crash can result in a serious injury, are breathtaking.

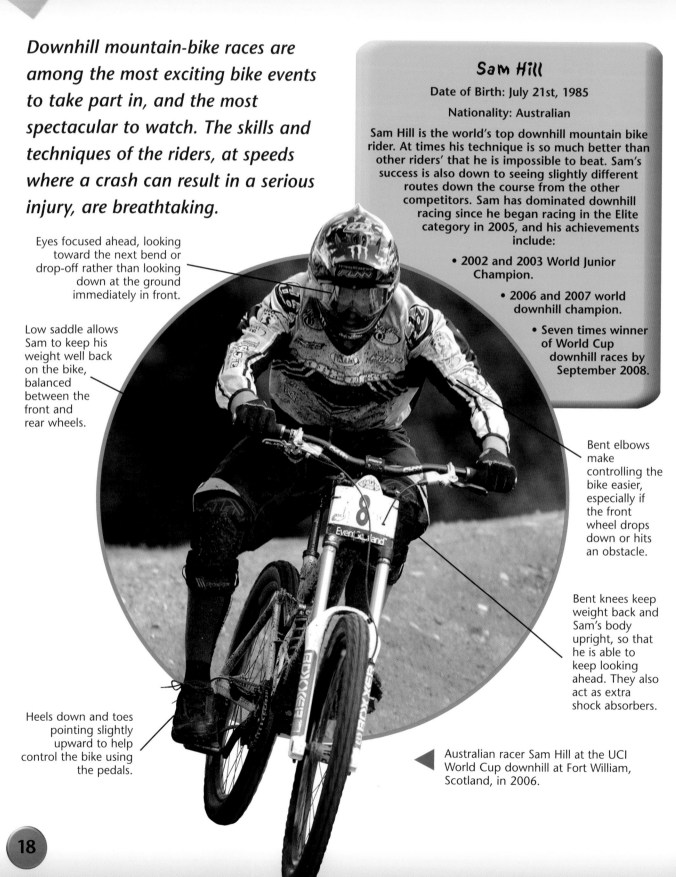

Sam Hill

Date of Birth: July 21st, 1985

Nationality: Australian

Sam Hill is the world's top downhill mountain bike rider. At times his technique is so much better than other riders' that he is impossible to beat. Sam's success is also down to seeing slightly different routes down the course from the other competitors. Sam has dominated downhill racing since he began racing in the Elite category in 2005, and his achievements include:

- 2002 and 2003 World Junior Champion.
- 2006 and 2007 world downhill champion.
- Seven times winner of World Cup downhill races by September 2008.

Eyes focused ahead, looking toward the next bend or drop-off rather than looking down at the ground immediately in front.

Low saddle allows Sam to keep his weight well back on the bike, balanced between the front and rear wheels.

Bent elbows make controlling the bike easier, especially if the front wheel drops down or hits an obstacle.

Bent knees keep weight back and Sam's body upright, so that he is able to keep looking ahead. They also act as extra shock absorbers.

Heels down and toes pointing slightly upward to help control the bike using the pedals.

Australian racer Sam Hill at the UCI World Cup downhill at Fort William, Scotland, in 2006.

The point where the two edges of the road or tail appear to meet is called the "vanishing point." Expert riders use the vanishing point as a way of judging their speed.

Vanishing point

Key Skills
The same key skills used by downhill racers can be learned and used by other cyclists. These skills fall into three main areas:

1) Body position
The key skill here is to keep your weight far back on the bike. Some riders even hang their bottom off the seat, resting their stomach on it instead. This makes it less likely that they can be thrown over the handlebars, and gives a more streamlined riding position.

2) Cornering
The "vanishing point" (see the photo above) can help you to judge the right speed into a corner. If the vanishing point is moving closer, slow down. If it is moving away, speed up.

3) Braking
Brake smoothly. The front brake is more powerful, but it is important to use some back brake as well, or the rear wheel will lift up and tip you off.

Ollies

Ollies, or jumps, are a key part of every BMX rider's set of skills, whether doing tricks or racing. They can also be useful for other kinds of cyclist.

BMX

Ollies are the basis of many BMX tricks on street or ramp. Ollies are also a key skill for BMX racers, who steer their bikes around a dirt track that has banked curves called berms, tight curves, and tabletops (steep ramps with a raised, flat area of earth between them). Being able to ollie your bike over these, instead of riding on them, gives racers a big advantage.

Non-BMX riders

Being able to ollie is useful for mountain bikers, who often have to get over tree

1 Standing up on the pedals, give one of them a hard push while pulling up on the handlebars. The front wheel will rise off the ground.

2 Bring your weight forward and roll your wrists forward slightly. This will bring the back wheel up into the air as well. (If you're wearing clipless pedals or toeclips, these make lifting the back wheel a lot easier.)

roots, logs, rocks and other obstacles. Even road riders benefit from knowing how to ollie, as long as they are completely expert at it. Most roads have a good selection of curbs, drainage covers, manholes, and other obstacles, and being able to do a little jump to lift your wheels clear of these can be very useful.

Elite BMX rider, Great Britain's Shanaze Reade, competes in a qualifying moto at the Juan de Fuca Recreation Center before the start of the 2007 UCI BMX World Championships in Canada, in 2007.

3 *Keeping your balance, land the bike either back wheel first or both wheels together. (It's dangerous to land on the front wheel because you almost always get flipped over the handlebars.) Ride away wearing a big grin.*

Shanaze Reade

Date of Birth: September 23rd, 1988

Nationality: British

Shanaze Reade became one of the world's top BMX racers when she won a junior world championship in 2006. She then won a senior world championship the next year. In 2008 she won the gold medal in the World BMX Championships in China. Showing that she's highly versatile, Shanaze is also a top track cyclist. In 2007 and 2008 she won a world team sprint championship, riding with Victoria Pendleton. (Victoria is another of Britain's top riders, and a world individual sprint champion.)

Riding High

The world's highest aerial on a bike was performed by legendary BMX ramp rider American Mat Hoffman. He launched his bike more than 50 feet (15m) into the air, and landed safely.

Road racing first became popular in the early 1900s. Today, road races take many forms, and usually involving cycling from place to place with a group of other riders.

Race Distances

There are several different distances of road race. Some last just a few hours. In short races such as these, the first rider across the line wins. Other races, called stage races, go on for days. In these multiday events, the rider with the fastest overall time wins.

Time Trials

Time trails are a bike race against the clock. Time trialing in Britain started because racing bicycles on open roads was not allowed until 1942. Cyclists began to organize secret events, where they would set off one after the other along a pre-determined route. The winner was the rider who finished the route in the fastest time. This is still how time trials work today.

Sportives

Bike events called sportives are growing increasingly popular among non-competition road cyclists. Groups of riders follow a set route, sometimes over several days. Sportives are not strictly competitions, but because they're timed, people do race each other. They are open to riders of most ages and abilities.

Great Britain's Nicole Cooke takes part in the Olympic women's cycling time trial in Athens in 2004.

Nicole Cooke

Date of Birth: April 13th, 1983

Nationality: British

Nicole Cooke is the most successful female British road racer ever. She won Britain's first gold medal of the Beijing Olympics in 2008 in a thrilling race. Other achievements include:

• Winning the overall Women's World Cup series in 2003 and 2006.

• Four world junior cycling championship gold medals, in road racing (twice), time trial, and cross-country mountain bike.

1 Road riders use a "chain gang" like this one to cover ground fast. The rider in front keeps up the pace, while those behind have an easier ride in his slipstream.

2 After his turn in front, the rider drops to the back of the group for a slight rest. A new rider takes over at the front. The first rider slowly makes his way back up the line as others take a turn at the front and drop back.

Only the rider's head and shoulders create air resistance.

Chest and stomach are parallel to the ground.

Hands on the "dropped" part of the handlebars.

Bent back keeps the rider's front low down.

Racers try to hold a good, fast aerodynamic position.

Track Racing

Track racing, like road racing, has been around for more than 100 years. Racers ride on customized oval tracks with banked bends. The racing is spectacular, and in some track events crashes are common.

Track Bikes

Track bikes are usually fixed-wheel. This means they have only one gear, and the rider's legs keep turning all the time the back wheel is going around. Track bikes do not have brakes, and the only way to slow down is to pedal more slowly. Riding one for the first time feels a bit like being on a runaway train!

Track Events

There is a huge variety of track events. These are the main ones:

• Sprint

Two riders start together, with the aim of crossing the line first. They do not go fast right from the start. In fact, they sometimes end up balancing motionless on their bikes, or barely moving at all! This is because it's

Track Start

1 *The racer gets into position, with the front wheel of the bike on the line. Either an assistant comes and grips the back wheel between his legs, or the bike is positioned with its back wheel in an automatic starting machine. With the bike held solid, the rider clips his shoes into the pedals.*

2 *The starting signal goes off and the rear wheel is released. The rider stands up on the pedals in order to get up to speed as quickly as possible.*

During team time-trial events, the riders use a similar chain-gang technique to the one shown on page 23.

Practice makes perfect, especially at the track—getting used to riding a track bike on the oval circuit before you race is crucial. ▶

much easier to win coming from behind, so each rider tries to go as slowly as possible until the very last moment, so that they get to go at the back.

• Pursuit
In the team pursuit, two teams of four riders start on opposite sides of the track. The fastest goes through to the next round. The individual pursuit has one rider on each side.

•Time trial
This is a flat-out race where the fastest time wins. It is raced over 1 km (0.6 miles) for men and 500 meters (0.3 miles) for women.

Murphy's Mile

The first cyclist ever to ride a mile in a minute was Charles Minthorn Murphy of the USA. He managed a time of 57.8 seconds in 1899—cycling behind a train, on a special boarded-in track!

Off-Road Racing

There are two main forms of off-road racing: cyclocross and mountain biking. Of these, cyclocross is older, and mountain biking more popular.

CycloCross

Cyclocross first became popular as a way for road riders to stay in shape in winter, when it was difficult to train on the roads. Today it is a full-blown competitive event. Sometimes riders race around a circuit for a set period of time, often an hour, with the one who goes farthest winning. Sometimes the race is over a set distance, with the winner being the first one over the line.

Mountain Biking

There are three main types of mountain-bike racing:
1) Cross-country, usually called XC, which is like a one-day road race but off-road.

The mass start of a 24-hour mountain-bike race. Look how far back the line of riders stretches.

2) Downhill, a timed run down a set course, a little like ski racing.

3) 4x or dual, where riders race side-by-side down a technical course.

Each of these requires specialized bikes and skills. Many racers ride both downhill and 4x, but at the top level none mix XC with either of the other two. XC racers have more in common with road riders, with the emphasis on endurance and sprinting power, rather than bike-handling skills.

24-Hour Racing

Twenty-four-hour racing is increasingly popular with nonprofessional riders. These are off-road races that last a day and a night. The winner is the person or team who manages the most whole laps in 24 hours. People enter either solo or as a relay team of two or four riders. At most 24-hour races there is a party atmosphere, with as much emphasis on having fun as winning.

A typical modern cross-country hardtail mountain bike (with front suspension but no rear): a steel frame, 110-mm (4.3-in) travel forks (which can move up to 110 mm (4.3in) to absorb shocks), wide handlebars, and 27 gears for dealing with just about any hill.

Mechanical skills are important for all bike racers, but especially mountain bikers, whose bikes take a lot of punishment during a race.

World Records and Champions

Road Racing

This table shows the riders with the most wins in the "Grand Tours" (the Tour de France, the Giro d' Italia in Italy, and the Vuelta e España in Spain):

Name:	Total wins:	Tour:	Giro:	Vuelta:
Eddy Merckx (Belgium, b.1945)	11	5	5	1
Bernard Hinault (France, b.1954)	10	5	3	2
Jacques Anquetil (France, 1934-87)	8	5	2	1
Fausto Coppi (Italy, 1919–60)	7	2	5	0
Miguel Indurain (Spain, b.1964)	7	5	2	0
Lance Armstrong, USA (b. 1971)	7	7	0	0
Gino Bartali (Italy, 1914–2000)	5	2	3	0
Alfredo Binda (Italy, 1902–86)	5	0	5	0
Felice Gimondi (Italy, b.1942)	5	1	3	1
Tony Rominger (Switzerland, b.1961)	4	0	1	3

Track Cycling

This table shows world record-holders as they stood in early 2008 and the year in which they set their record.

Event:	Rider and country:	Year:
Men's sprint	Curtis Harnett, CANADA	1993
Women's sprint	Olga Slusareva, RUSSIA	1996
Men's individual pursuit	Chris Boardman, GREAT BRITAIN	2004
Women's individual pursuit	Sarah Ulmer, NEW ZEALAND	2001
Men's 1-km time trial	Arnaud Tournant, FRANCE	2004
Women's 500-m time trial	Anna Meares, AUSTRALIA	2004
Men's team pursuit	AUSTRALIA 1995	2004

Mountain Biking

This table shows the riders with the most cross-country racing wins at world mountain bike championships (as of early 2008):

Men's:	Wins:
1 Julien Absalon, FRANCE	4
2 Henrik Djernis, DENMARK	3
3 Roland Green, CANADA	2
4 Thomas Frischknecht, SWITZERLAND	1
5 Filip Meirhaeghe , BELGIUM	1
6 Bart Brentjens, NETHERLANDS	1
7 Ned Overend, USA	1
8 John Tomac, USA	1

Women's:	Wins:
1 Gunn-Rita Dahle, NORWAY	4
2 Alison Sydor, CANADA	3
3 Paola Pezzo, ITALY	2
4 Margraita Fullana, SPAIN	2
5 Ruthie Matthes, USA	1
6 Sabine Spitz, GERMANY	1
7= Silvia Furst, SWITZERLAND	1
7= Irina Kalentieva, RUSSIA	1

Glossary and Websites

Aerodynamic Designed to reduce air resistance and so increase speed.

Air resistance Slowing-down effect of air on a moving object. If you stick your fingertips of the window out of a moving car, what you feel pushing on them is air resistance.

Banked Built to be steep-sided. A banked turn is built up on the outside so that it forces the bike and rider to lean over.

Berms Banked turns.

Clipless pedals Pedals that attach to special cycling shoes, and which you can only take off your feet by twisting the shoe sideways.

Cycle lane A special lane set aside for cyclists only to use.

Digestive To do with the digestion (breaking down inside the body) of food.

Drop-off Steep, sudden, and sometimes vertical descent on a mountain-bike trail.

Endurance The ability to do something for a long time.

Level A tube of liquid with an air bubble in the middle. When the air bubble is in the center of the tube, it means the tube is perfectly level.

Pollution Harmful substances such as gases released by vehicles, which cause damage to the environment.

Reflective Shining brightly when hit by light.

Shifts Changes or moves. In cycling, "shifting" means either changing gear or moving very fast.

Slipstream A pocket of still air behind another rider, where there is less air resistance to fight against.

Stages Parts. In a stage race, cyclists ride a set route each day, and each day's riding is one "stage."

Tabletops Steep slopes with a raised, flat area in between.

Time trials Races against the clock.

Toeclips Devices attached to pedals, which a rider's toes go inside to give them extra grip.

Websites

www.usacycling.org
Going online and joining USA Cycling allows you to race or ride your bike in one or more of USA Cycling's 2,500 sanctioned races and fun rides. The site also helps you locate bike clubs near you simply by clicking on your state.

www.letour.fr/indexus.html
The home site of the world's most popular bike race, the Tour de France. Here you can find out the route the Tour is taking each year, the teams and riders involved, and the history of the race.

www.uci.ch
The website of the Union Cycliste Internationale, the world governing body for cycling. The site has information about the different competition cycling events, plus results from competitions around the world.

www.nbl.org
The National Bicycle League promotes BMX cycling through its championship series, competitions, news, results, TV schedules and *BMX Today* magazine. The National Bicycle League also has their own large network of BMX Tracks across the country.

Index